COOKING
THE
ISRAELI
WAY

To Hanna, my favorite daughter

Copyright © 2002 by Lerner Publications Company

Lerner Publications Company
A division of Lerner Publishing Group
241 First Avenue North
Minneapolis, MN 55401 U.S.A.

Website address: www.lernerbooks.com

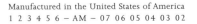
Library of Congress Cataloging-in-Publication Data

Bacon, Josephine.
    Cooking the Israeli way / by Josephine Bacon—Rev. & expanded
      p. cm. — (Easy menu ethnic cookbooks)
    Summary: An introduction to the cooking of Israel including such traditional recipes as cheese blintzes, shakshooka, felafel in pita, and poppyseed cake. Also includes information on the geography, customs, and people of the Middle Eastern country.
    ISBN 0-8225-4112-2 (lib. bdg. : alk. paper)
    1. Cookery, Israeli—Juvenile literature. 2. Israel—Social life and customs—Juvenile literature. [1. Cookery, Israeli. 2. Israel—Social life and customs.] I. Title. II. Series.
TX724 .B225 2002   2001006819
641.595694—dc21

Manufactured in the United States of America
1 2 3 4 5 6 – AM – 07 06 05 04 03 02

COOKING

revised and expanded

THE

to include new low-fat

ISRAELI

and vegetarian recipes

WAY

Josephine Bacon

Lerner Publications Company • Minneapolis

Contents

Introduction

Israel is a country with a very unusual heritage. It is the ancient land of the Bible, the setting for the events described in the scriptures sacred to both Jews and Christians. Because of this biblical connection, the names of Israel's cities—Jerusalem, Haifa, Bethlehem, and Nazareth—may be as familiar to many Americans as the names of cities in the United States. At the same time, Israel is a very new nation, established in 1948 as a homeland for Jews from all parts of the world—the only country in the world where Judaism is the major religion and where most of the population is Jewish.

The food of Israel is as unique as the history of the country. It is a blend of many different cooking traditions, combining influences of the Middle East with those from many parts of Europe and the United States. The result is a wonderful blend of flavors.

Delight your holiday guests with this glazed poppy seed cake. (Recipe on page 50.)

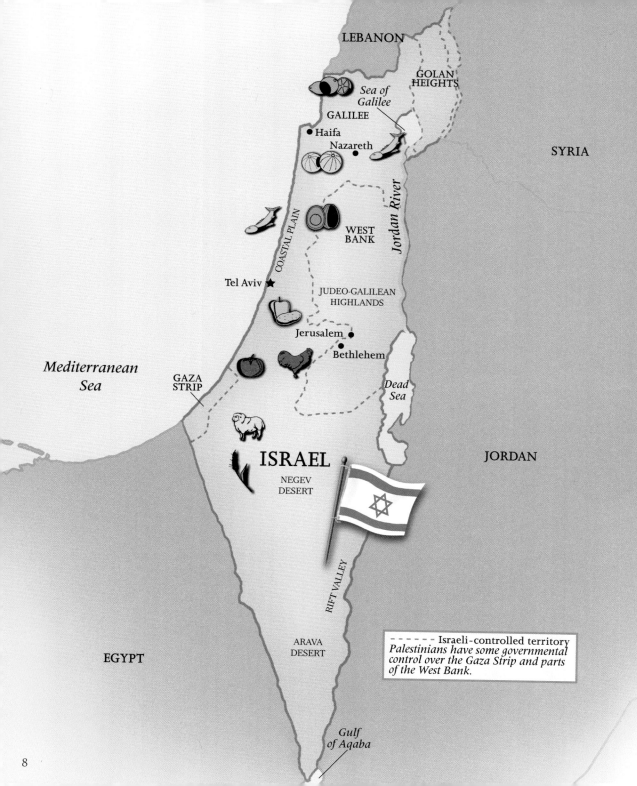

LEBANON

GOLAN
HEIGHTS

*Sea of
Galilee*

GALILEE

SYRIA

● Haifa
Nazareth ●

WEST
BANK

Jordan River

COASTAL PLAIN

Tel Aviv ★

JUDEO-GALILEAN
HIGHLANDS

Jerusalem ●

Bethlehem ●

*Mediterranean
Sea*

GAZA
STRIP

*Dead
Sea*

JORDAN

ISRAEL

NEGEV
DESERT

EGYPT

RIFT VALLEY

ARAVA
DESERT

- - - - - Israeli-controlled territory
*Palestinians have some governmental
control over the Gaza Strip and parts
of the West Bank.*

*Gulf
of Aqaba*

The Land and Its People

Israel is a very small country, only one-fourth the size of the state of Maine. It occupies a narrow strip of land 265 miles (424 kilometers) long at the eastern end of the Mediterranean Sea. The climate of the country resembles that of southern California. Except at higher elevations, where it is often cold enough to snow, Israel has hot, dry summers and short, mild winters.

The northernmost part of Israel, Upper Galilee, is mountainous. Lower Galilee is a fertile plain bordering the Sea of Galilee, which is actually a large freshwater lake with a few saltwater wells in it. The Jordan River connects the Sea of Galilee with a true saltwater lake, the Dead Sea, which is the saltiest body of water in the world. It is also the lowest point on the face of the earth—1,310 feet (399 meters) below sea level.

The central part of Israel is the most fertile, especially the area of the Coastal Plain called the Plain of Sharon. Most Israelis live in the Coastal Plain, and most of the nation's agriculture and industry are located there. To the east of the Coastal Plain lie the Judeo-Galilean Highlands, with historic Jerusalem standing atop one of the high, rolling hills. To the south is the Negev Desert, whose dry soil is quite fertile when irrigated. Farther south, the land drops sharply away to the Arava, a desert much like California's Death Valley, where the climate is so dry and the earth so salty that very little will grow there.

Like the United States, Israel has a population made up largely of immigrants or descendants of immigrants. Only a small minority of present-day Israelis lived in the country before it gained independence in 1948.

In the late 1800s, Jews first began returning to the region then called Palestine, the site of their historic homeland in the Middle East. These early immigrants, known as Zionists, were determined to establish a Jewish state in the area, a state where all Jews would be guaranteed entry and safety from persecution. Most of the earliest settlers came from Russia and Poland, but Zionist movements soon sprang up all over Europe and in the United States. Small numbers of Jews from these areas also found their way to Palestine. After Palestine was partitioned and the state of Israel was established in 1948, the Jewish population of the new nation doubled in size.

The approximately six million Jews who live in modern Israel have come from almost every country in the world. Among them are refugees who fled Europe during World War II (1939–1945) to escape the Nazi plan to exterminate Jews. Others came from Arab countries of the Middle East where hostility toward Jews increased greatly after the establishment of the state of Israel. More recently, immigrants have come from Russia and Ethiopia.

About 83 percent of the people of Israel are Jewish, but there is a large Muslim population in cities such as Nazareth and Galilee. Other minorities, including Druses (an Arabic-speaking people of

Lively nightlife on the streets of Israel appeals to its cultural mix.

the Middle East who practice a secret religion related to Islam) and Armenian Christians, also live there. Jerusalem, which is a holy city for Muslims, Christians, and Jews, is home to members of all three religious groups.

It has not been easy for Israel to make one nation out of people from so many different regions and cultures. Israel has two official languages—Hebrew, the language spoken by most of the Jewish population, and Arabic, spoken mainly by the Arabs. Hebrew has changed to some extent over the centuries, but in the twenty-first century, an Israeli can read the original Hebrew words of the Bible almost as easily as the daily newspaper.

The army is a unifying element for Israelis. Because of its conflicts with neighboring states, Israel maintains a strong military. Almost all young people spend time in the military—men three years and women two years—when they reach the age of eighteen. Israel's army is a great melting pot, bringing together people of different backgrounds who would most likely never have met in civilian life.

The Food

Israel's cuisine is as diverse as its people and reflects a combination of influences from all over the world. Because most of the country's population is Jewish, one of the strongest of these influences is the religious and cultural tradition shared by Jews everywhere.

The traditional dietary laws observed by Orthodox Jews have a strong influence on Israeli cooking. These dietary laws require that all food be kosher, which means "fit" or "proper." Orthodox Jews do not eat pork, shellfish, or meat from certain other animals, such as rabbits. They also follow strict rules regarding the slaughtering of animals and the preparation of meat for human consumption. Another dietary law forbids eating dairy products and meat at the same meal. Orthodox Jewish households and all Israel's public

Jewish men select stalks of four species of plants—palm, willow, citron, and myrtle—for ceremonial use during the eight-day harvest festival, Sukkot.

institutions observe the dietary laws, serving kosher food and maintaining separate cooking utensils, tableware, and dishwashing facilities for milk and meat dishes.

Israeli cuisine has been shaped not only by Jewish tradition but also by the climate and the geography of the country. The kinds of food grown and readily available in Israel are often featured in Israeli menus. For example, high-quality fruits and vegetables, which are abundant and inexpensive, can be found at nearly every meal. Like many other countries of the Middle East, Israel also produces and consumes a wide variety of dairy products.

In general, Israelis eat less meat than most Americans and Europeans do. This is due partly to the demands of the dietary laws, which forbid the consumption of many parts of animals, and partly to the dry climate and lack of grazing land. While turkey and chicken are inexpensive in Israel, red meat is very costly and the quality is poor by U.S. standards. Because of the scarcity of meat, some Israelis limit their diets to vegetables, fruits, and dairy products, although some are vegetarians because of health reasons or a concern for animal welfare.

Holidays and Festivals

People in Israel observe holidays and festivals throughout the year. Many of the holidays are based on the Hebrew (Jewish) lunar calendar rather than the Western Gregorian calendar, which is based on the solar year from January through December. In addition, all holidays begin at sundown. Special foods traditionally associated with each holiday are prepared in homes throughout the land and are often sold by street vendors.

Rosh Hashanah (the Jewish New Year) takes place in September or October, rather than in January. Israelis celebrate the New Year with sweet foods, such as apples and honey cake. At the beginning of the Rosh Hashanah meal, an apple is dipped in honey. The honey symbolizes the hope for a sweet year. Another symbolic food for Rosh Hashanah is the round challah (bread), symbol of life, which can also be prepared as a sweet bread.

Ten days after Rosh Hashanah, on Yom Kippur (the Day of Atonement), no food or drink is allowed for twenty-six hours—from sundown to sundown. This solemn day is followed by an eight-day harvest festival called Sukkot (the Feast of the Tabernacles). In ancient times, this festival celebrated the successful harvest of the previous year with the actual reaping of crops and fruits and the picking of grapes and olives. Symbolically, the festival marks the arrival of the people of Israel in the Holy Land. Dishes featuring seasonal fruits and vegetables—symbols of plenty—are eaten.

Around Christmastime in December, Israelis—and Jews around the world—celebrate Hanukkah (the Festival of Lights, also called Chanukah). In 165 B.C., Jews regained control of the city of Jerusalem and cleaned and rededicated their temple. According to tradition, a vessel was found with enough oil to burn for one day, but it miraculously burned for eight. In modern times, Jews celebrate this eight-day holiday each night by lighting an additional candle in a special candelabra called a menorah. After the candle ceremony, families sing songs, play with spinning tops called dreidels, open presents, and eat fried foods, including potato pancakes (*latkes* or *levivot*) and doughnuts (*sufganiah*). Foods fried in oil are a reminder of the ancient oil lamp.

In late January or early February, Israelis eat fruit and plant trees on Tu B'Shevat (the New Year of Trees), similar to Arbor Day in the United States and Canada. In Israel, the white and pink blossoms of the almond trees are in full bloom during the holiday.

The favorite festival of children is Purim (the Feast of Esther). According to the biblical story, Esther was a valiant Jewish queen who prevented the massacre of her people in ancient Persia. In early spring, many towns hold street festivals. Although Purim is a normal workday in Israel, in the evening after the workday, children and adults have parties. They parade through the streets in costumes and eat sweet cookies filled with poppy seeds or prunes. These treats, called Haman's Ears or Haman's Pockets (depending on their size), are named after the villain in the story of Esther.

Pesach (Passover) is the main spring festival. Nothing leavened with yeast may be eaten during this seven-day festival. Matzo, a flat, unleavened, crackerlike bread, replaces yeast bread in homes, hotels, and restaurants, and no leavened bread is sold in Jewish stores. Passover is often preceded by vigorous spring cleaning to remove all traces of leavened bread and related products from homes. On the first evening of Passover, a festive, ritual meal called the Seder is

Israeli youth perform a dance for Purim on a temporary stage in Jerusalem.

served. The meal commemorates the escape of the Jews from Egyptian bondage in ancient biblical times. The story is read from a book called the Haggadah. While the Haggadah is read, a Seder plate sits on the table. The plate contains the traditional Passover foods: three matzos; a roasted egg; a leg of lamb (or a bone) to symbolize the lamb that was sacrificed at Passover in ancient times; salt water to symbolize the tears shed by the people of Israel during their slavery; a bitter herb (usually horseradish) to represent the bitterness of slavery; a green vegetable (usually parsley or lettuce) to represent new life and growth; and haroset, a delicious fruit-and-nut paste that is eaten with matzo, to symbolize the mortar Jewish slaves used when they built cities in Egypt. Four ritual glasses of wine are drunk during the meal, and a goblet is set in the middle of the table for the prophet Elijah, who Jews believe will bring the promised Messiah. The Seder can last for several hours, but it must end by midnight.

Three other springtime holidays include Yom Hasho'ah (Holocaust Memorial Day), Yom Hazikaron (Memorial Day), and Yom Ha'atzma (Independence Day). On Holocaust Memorial Day, special services take place at Yad Vashem Holocaust Memorial in Jerusalem and elsewhere in the country. Entertainment venues are closed, and at 11:00 A.M., everyone stands silent as sirens sound in memory of the six million Jews who were killed by the Nazis during World War II. Memorial Day is a day of mourning for those Israelis who died in war. Ceremonies are held around the country, entertainment sites are closed, and, again, at 11:00 A.M., sirens sound in memory of the fallen. Independence Day marks the day in May 1948 when Israel achieved independence as a nation. The exact date of Yom Ha'atzma follows the Hebrew calendar. Although gala events, fireworks, and military parades take place throughout the country, most Israelis go picnicking or swimming.

The last festival of the Jewish calendar, Shavout (the Feast of Weeks), occurs in May or early June and lasts for eight days. It is also called Hag Habikkurim (the Festival of the First Fruits) and marks the harvest of the first summer fruits and vegetables. According to tradition, the festival celebrates the day on which Moses received the Torah (the law) on Mount Sinai. On this holiday, it is customary to eat meatless meals with an emphasis on dairy products, such as cheese pancakes and a cone-shaped cake representing Mount Sinai.

In addition to the yearly festivals and holidays, Israelis have a weekly holiday to celebrate Saturday, Sabbath or Shabbat (the Jewish Day of Rest), which begins at sundown on Friday night and ends at nightfall on Saturday. On Friday afternoon, the whole country winds down, and most Jewish businesses close until Saturday night or Sunday morning. In religious neighborhoods, people rush to finish cooking and cleaning before the Sabbath begins. Devout Israeli Jews do not cook, travel, answer the telephone, or use money or writing materials during the Sabbath. Some religious neighborhoods in Jerusalem are even closed to traffic. For religious Israelis, the Sabbath is a day of solemn services and family gatherings followed by singing and dancing. The Sabbath meal is a formal occasion. The table is laid with a white cloth and the best dishes and silverware are used. Unless the Sabbath falls during the week of Shavuot—the Feast of Weeks—when dairy products are traditionally eaten, or unless the family is vegetarian, some kind of meat dish is served in even the poorest households. Each Jewish family has its own special dishes for the Sabbath meal, which is prepared on Friday afternoon and then kept warm until the next day. Nonreligious Israelis, however, take to the roads to enjoy their holiday. In any case, good food is an essential part of the Sabbath celebrations, as it is in many aspects of Israeli life.

An Israeli Market

Throughout Israel, cooks enjoy a wealth of fresh fruits and vegetables grown in Israel's sunny climate. Colorful outdoor markets, called *souks*, display fresh oranges, red and green grapes, grapefruits and lemons, melons, tomatoes, avocados, figs, dates, peaches, apples, lettuce, potatoes, peppers, onions, peas, beans, carrots, cucumbers, cauliflower, deep purple eggplant, black, green, and purple olives, and beautiful bouquets of flowers. Shoppers can also buy fresh fish and poultry. After a morning of shopping, they might stop at one of the many street vendors selling a variety of delicious morsels—perhaps tasty felafel (mashed chickpeas that have been fried and wedged into pita bread, then topped with veggies and a savory sauce), freshly baked bagels, or sugary doughnuts. Israeli markets abound in delectable produce and tempting tidbits.

Before You Begin

Cooking any dish, plain or fancy, is easier and more fun if you are familiar with the ingredients and the preparation. Israeli cooking calls for some ingredients that you may not know. Sometimes special cookware is also used, although the recipes in this book can easily be prepared with ordinary utensils and pans.

The most important thing you need to know before you start is how to be a careful cook. On the following page, you'll find a few rules that will make your cooking experience safe, fun, and easy. Next, take a look at the "dictionary" of utensils, terms, and special ingredients. You may also want to read the section on preparing healthy, low-fat meals for yourself, your family, and your friends.

Once you've picked out a recipe to try, read through it from beginning to end. Now you are ready to shop for ingredients and to organize the cookware you will need. When you have assembled everything, you're ready to begin cooking.

Orange slices, cranberries, and dates make this refreshing Tu B'Shevat salad as flavorful as it is colorful. (Recipe on page 64.)

The Careful Cook

Whenever you cook, there are certain safety rules you must always keep in mind. Even experienced cooks follow these rules when they are in the kitchen.

- Always wash your hands before handling food. Thoroughly wash all raw vegetables and fruits to remove dirt, chemicals, and insecticides. Wash uncooked poultry, fish, and meat under cold water.
- Use a cutting board when cutting up vegetables and fruits. Don't cut them up in your hand! And be sure to cut in a direction *away* from you and your fingers.
- Long hair or loose clothing can easily catch fire if brought near the burners of a stove. If you have long hair, tie it back before you start cooking.
- Turn all pot handles toward the back of the stove so that you will not catch your sleeves or jewelry on them. This is especially important when younger brothers and sisters are around. They could easily knock off a pot and get burned.
- Always use a pot holder to steady hot pots or to take pans out of the oven. Don't use a wet cloth on a hot pan because the steam it produces could burn you.
- Lift the lid of a steaming pot with the opening away from you so that you will not get burned.
- If you get burned, hold the burn under cold running water. Do not put grease or butter on it. Cold water helps to take the heat out, but grease or butter will only keep it in.
- If grease or cooking oil catches fire, throw baking soda or salt at the bottom of the flame to put it out. (Water will *not* put out a grease fire.) Call for help, and try to turn all the stove burners to "off."

Cooking Utensils

colander—A bowl-shaped dish with holes in it that is used for washing or draining food

melon baller—A utensil with a small rounded end for scooping pieces from melons and other fleshy foods

sieve—A bowl-shaped utensil made of wire or plastic mesh used to wash or drain small, fine foods such as tea or rice

slotted spoon—A spoon with small openings in the bowl used to scoop solid food out of a liquid

spatula—A flat, thin utensil, usually metal, used to lift, toss, turn, or scoop up food

tongs—A utensil shaped either like tweezers or scissors with flat, blunt ends to grasp food

Cooking Terms

baste—To pour, brush, or spoon liquid over food as it cooks in order to flavor and moisten it

beat—To stir rapidly in a circular motion

boil—To heat a liquid over high heat until bubbles form and rise rapidly to the surface

brown—To cook food quickly in fat over high heat so that the surface turns an even brown

chop—To cut into small pieces

cream—To beat ingredients together until the mixture is smooth

garnish—To decorate with small pieces of food such as chopped parsley

grate—To cut into tiny pieces by rubbing the food against a grater

knead—To work dough by pressing it with the palms, pushing it outward, and then pressing it over on itself *mince*—To chop food into very small pieces

preheat—To allow an oven to warm up to a certain temperature before putting food in it

sauté—To fry quickly over high heat in oil or fat, stirring or turning the food to prevent burning

scald—To heat a liquid (such as milk) to a temperature just below its boiling point

shred—To tear or cut into small pieces, either by hand or with a grater

simmer—To cook over low heat in liquid kept just below its boiling point

Special Ingredients

allspice—The berry of a West Indian tree, used whole or ground, whose flavor resembles a combination of cinnamon, nutmeg, and cloves

balsamic vinegar—An aged Italian vinegar made from the juice of white grapes

chickpeas—A pale, round legume, available dried or canned. They are also called garbanzo beans.

chili powder—A mixture of ground chilies and other herbs and spices, including cumin and oregano

coriander—An herb used as a flavoring and as a decorative garnish. Fresh coriander is also called cilantro.

cumin seed—The seeds of an herb used to give food a pungent, slightly hot taste

dill—An herb with aromatic foliage and seeds used to flavor foods. Dried dill is also called dill weed.

felafel mix—A dry mix of chickpeas, flour, and spices

field beans—A variety of beans native to the Middle East. Often called Egyptian field beans, they are available at Middle Eastern stores, specialty stores, or some supermarkets.

fig—An oblong or pear-shaped fruit that grows on trees of the mulberry family

matzo—Crisp unleavened bread eaten mainly at Passover by Jews around the world

matzo meal—Finely ground matzos

olive oil—An oil made by pressing olives. It is used in cooking and for dressing salads.

paprika—A red seasoning made from ground dried pods of the capsicum pepper plant

pine nuts—The edible seed of certain pine trees

pita bread—A flat, round bread common throughout the Middle East. When baked, a puffed pocket of air forms in the center of pita bread.

tahini—A paste of ground sesame seeds, available canned or bottled

Healthy and Low-Fat Cooking Tips

Many modern cooks are concerned about preparing healthy, low-fat meals. Fortunately, there are simple ways to reduce the fat content of most dishes. Here are a few general tips for adapting the recipes in this book. Throughout the book, you'll also find specific suggestions for individual recipes—and don't worry, they'll still taste delicious!

Many recipes call for butter or oil to sauté vegetables or other ingredients. Using oil lowers saturated fat right away, but you can also reduce the amount of oil you use. Sprinkling a little salt on the vegetables brings out their natural juices, so less oil is needed. It's also a good idea to use a small, nonstick frying pan if you decide to use less oil than the recipe calls for.

Another common substitution for butter is margarine. Before making this substitution, consider the recipe. If it is a dessert, it's often best to use butter. Margarine may noticeably change the taste or consistency of the food.

Cheese is a common source of unwanted fat. Many cheeses are available in reduced or nonfat varieties, but keep in mind that these varieties often don't melt as well. Another easy way to reduce the amount of fat from cheese is simply to use less of it! To avoid losing flavor, you might try using a stronger-tasting cheese.

Some cooks like to replace ground beef with ground turkey to lower fat. However, since this does change the flavor, you may need to experiment a little bit to decide if you like this substitution. Buying extra-lean ground beef is also an easy way to reduce fat.

There are many ways to prepare meals that are good for you and still taste great. As you become a more experienced cook, try experimenting with recipes and substitutions to find the methods that work best for you.

METRIC CONVERSIONS

Cooks in the United States measure both liquid and solid ingredients using standard containers based on the 8-ounce cup and the tablespoon. These measurements are based on volume, while the metric system of measurement is based on both weight (for solids) and volume (for liquids). To convert from U.S. fluid tablespoons, ounces, quarts, and so forth to metric liters is a straightforward conversion, using the chart below. However, since solids have different weights—one cup of rice does not weigh the same as one cup of grated cheese, for example—many cooks who use the metric system have kitchen scales to weigh different ingredients. The chart below will give you a good starting point for basic conversions to the metric system.

MASS (weight)

1 ounce (oz.)	=	28.0 grams (g)
8 ounces	=	227.0 grams
1 pound (lb.) or 16 ounces	=	0.45 kilograms (kg)
2.2 pounds	=	1.0 kilogram

LIQUID VOLUME

1 teaspoon (tsp.)	=	5.0 milliliters (ml)
1 tablespoon (tbsp.)	=	15.0 milliliters
1 fluid ounce (oz.)	=	30.0 milliliters
1 cup (c.)	=	240 milliliters
1 pint (pt.)	=	480 milliliters
1 quart (qt.)	=	0.95 liters (l)
1 gallon (gal.)	=	3.80 liters

LENGTH

¼ inch (in.)	=	0.6 centimeters (cm)
½ inch	=	1.25 centimeters
1 inch	=	2.5 centimeters

TEMPERATURE

212°F	=	100°C (boiling point of water)
225°F	=	110°C
250°F	=	120°C
275°F	=	135°C
300°F	=	150°C
325°F	=	160°C
350°F	=	180°C
375°F	=	190°C
400°F	=	200°C

(To convert temperature in Fahrenheit to Celsius, subtract 32 and multiply by .56)

PAN SIZES

8-inch cake pan	=	20 x 4-centimeter cake pan
9-inch cake pan	=	23 x 3.5-centimeter cake pan
11 x 7-inch baking pan	=	28 x 18-centimeter baking pan
13 x 9-inch baking pan	=	32.5 x 23-centimeter baking pan
9 x 5-inch loaf pan	=	23 x 13-centimeter loaf pan
2-quart casserole	=	2-liter casserole

An Israeli Table

For holidays, an Israeli table is adorned with the best tablecloth, the finest china and crystal, and the household's good silverware. Around the table are family members and close friends who have come together to celebrate while sharing delicious food, good conversation, and ancient traditions.

The foods of Israel are a blend of many cultures. They have been modified by modern ingredients, utensils, dietary concerns, and cooking methods, yet they also reflect the unique bounty of the land and the ancient practices and traditions of its people.

Family meals are a feature of Israelis' weekly holiday, the Sabbath or Shabbat (the Jewish Day of Rest), which begins at sundown on Friday and ends at nightfall on Saturday.

An Israeli Menu

Below are menu plans for a typical Israeli breakfast and lunch (often the main meal of the day), together with shopping lists of items that you will need to prepare these meals.* All the recipes are found in this book.

BREAKFAST

Israeli salad

Egg and tomato scramble

Fresh fruit

SHOPPING LIST:

Produce

2 tomatoes
1 cucumber
1 green pepper
1 bunch parsley
1 lemon
fresh fruit of choice

Dairy/Egg

1 stick butter or margarine
3 eggs

Canned/Bottled/Boxed

olive oil
1 14½-oz. can peeled, whole tomatoes

Miscellaneous

salt
pepper
chili powder
flour
pita bread

*If you plan to do a lot of Israeli cooking, you may want to stock up on some of the items on these shopping lists and keep them on hand. Garlic, olive oil, felafel mix, and tahini all keep well and are common ingredients in many Israeli dishes.

LUNCH

Tu B'Shevat salad

Baked fish

Potato pancakes

Melon dessert

SHOPPING LIST:

Produce

1 orange
1 avocado
2 small cantaloupes
½ lb. seedless green grapes
½ lb. seedless red grapes
4 peaches
1 endive
1 bunch watercress
½ head romaine lettuce
2 dates
dried cranberries
1 head garlic
2 onions
1 medium tomato
6 white potatoes
1 lemon
1 bunch fresh dill

Dairy/Egg

4 eggs
8 oz. sour cream
1 stick butter or margarine

Meat/Fish/Poultry

2 lb. fish fillets—flounder,
   sole, or haddock

Canned/Bottled/Boxed

applesauce
matzo meal or flour
balsamic vinegar
olive oil
Dijon mustard
white grape juice

Miscellaneous

salt
pepper
cinnamon
baking powder
sugar

Breakfast / Arukhat Boker

Breakfasts in Israel are hearty, especially in the countryside where they are eaten at the crack of dawn before a hard day's work in the fields. On Saturday, the Sabbath, when no cooking is permitted in Orthodox Jewish households, the meal is a hearty brunch of cold foods such as olives, yogurt, breads, jams, various cheeses, and smoked and pickled fish. It is accompanied by lots of hot tea or coffee from a samovar (an urn with a spigot at its base and a device for heating its contents) that is kept on the boil from Friday evening to Saturday dusk.

Garnish this savory egg and tomato scramble with a pinwheel of freshly cut tomato slices and a sprig of parsley. (Recipe on page32.)

Egg and Tomato Scramble/ Shakshooka

Tunisian Jews, who like very spicy food, brought this dish to Israel. The amount of chili powder can be increased or decreased, depending on how hot you like your food. Like most Israeli break- fast dishes, shakshooka can be served at any meal. The tomato mixture can be made in advance and reheated before adding the eggs.

1 14½-oz. can whole peeled
 tomatoes

¼ c. butter or margarine

1 tsp. chili powder

1 tbsp. all-purpose flour

3 eggs

½ tsp. salt

pita bread

1. Place tomatoes in a colander and drain well. Transfer tomatoes to a bowl and break into small pieces with a spoon.

2. Melt butter or margarine in a deep skillet or saucepan on low heat. Add tomatoes, chili powder, and flour and stir until smooth.

3. Simmer gently, uncovered, for 1 hour, stirring occasionally.

4. In a small bowl, beat together eggs and salt. Just before serving, add eggs to tomato mixture and stir lightly, cooking until eggs are set. Serve hot with pita bread.

Preparation time: 10 minutes
Cooking time: 1¼ hours
Serves 4

Israeli Salad/ Salat Yisraeli

Salad is eaten at almost every Israeli meal. On the kibbutz (collective community), oil, lemon juice, and a bowl of whole vegetables are left on each table, and diners make their own individual salads so that they are absolutely fresh.

2 tomatoes, chopped

I cucumber, peeled and chopped

I green pepper, seeded and chopped

4 tbsp. chopped fresh parsley

2 tbsp. olive oil

juice of I lemon (about 3 tbsp.)

½ tsp. salt

¼ tsp. pepper

1. In a large bowl, combine chopped tomatoes, cucumber, green pepper, and parsley. Sprinkle with olive oil and toss.

2. Add lemon juice, salt, and pepper to salad and toss again. Serve immediately.

Preparation time: 20 minutes
Serves 4

Snacks / Mata'amim

Israelis are busy people and they have made an art form out of stand-up dining. If it's edible, someone in Israel has found a way to eat it in a pita bread without dripping on their clothing.

Urbanites start work early in the morning. Offices are open at 8:00 A.M., and workers eat lunch rather late, around 1:00 P.M. Snacking gives Israelis the energy they need to keep up their hectic pace.

Street food stands, rolling carts, and modest eateries are plentiful. Their services are perhaps most in demand on Fridays. Weekly sabbath observances shorten the workweek and ensure a particular dependence on snacks during the headlong rush to prepare for this weekly holiday.

Pita stuffed with felafel, colorful peppers, and cucumbers, makes an attractive, convenient, and complete meal for busy people on the go. (Recipe on page 37.)

Israeli Doughnuts / Soofganiyot

Doughnuts are a favorite seasonal snack, eaten mostly in winter at Hanukkah. These doughnuts, cooked in oil, commemorate the oil that burned in the ruined temple in Jerusalem for eight days, although the supply appeared to be enough only for a single day. The secret of a really delicious doughnut is its freshness, so fry these just before serving. The dough can be made well ahead of time and refrigerated until ready to use.

2½ c. all-purpose flour

1 tsp. baking powder

2 eggs, beaten

1½ c. (12 oz.) sour cream

2 tbsp. sugar

¼ tsp. salt

1 tsp. vanilla extract

1¼ c. vegetable oil (for frying)

1 c. powdered sugar (for coating doughnuts)

1. In a mixing bowl, add each ingredient (except oil and powdered sugar) one at a time, mixing well after each addition. The batter will be very soft.

2. In a deep skillet, heat oil until hot enough to fry a 1-inch cube of bread in 1 minute. Carefully place dough, 1 tablespoon at a time, into oil. Fry doughnuts, a few at a time, 3 to 5 minutes, or until golden brown on all sides. Remove from oil with slotted spoon and drain on paper towels.

3. When all doughnuts are fried, pour powdered sugar into a plastic or brown paper bag. Add a few doughnuts at a time, close bag, and shake gently, until well coated. Repeat until all doughnuts are coated with sugar. Serve warm.

Preparation time: 20 minutes
Cooking time: 15 minutes
Makes about 25 doughnuts

Felafel in Pita/Felafel Bipita

Sidewalk food and drink sellers are common throughout the Middle East, and many of the snacks they sell are meals in themselves. Felafel, considered Israel's national dish, is one such nutritious and filling food.

1 10-oz. package felafel mix

1¼ c. vegetable oil (for frying)

1 tomato, chopped

½ cucumber, chopped

½ green pepper, seeded and chopped

¼ small head lettuce, shredded

4 pieces pita bread

4 tbsp. tahini, thinned according to directions on can

1. Prepare felafel mix according to package directions. Roll into small balls about the size of walnuts.

2. In a deep skillet, heat oil over medium-high heat until hot. Carefully place balls of felafel into oil, a few at a time, and fry 3 to 5 minutes until golden brown on all sides. Remove from oil with slotted spoon and drain on paper towels.

3. In a medium bowl, combine tomato, cucumber, green pepper, and lettuce.

4. Cut each piece of pita bread in half. Into the pocket of each pita, put 3 felafel balls and 2 to 3 tbsp. salad mixture. Dribble 1 tbsp. tahini into each. Serve immediately.

Preparation time: 30 minutes
Cooking time: 10 minutes
Serves 4

Hummus

The word hummus means "chickpea" in both Hebrew and Arabic. Hummus establishments, usually hole-in-the-wall joints, abound in Israel, and many Israelis frequent their own favorite spots.

1 c. dried chickpeas*

1 c. tahini

½ c. lemon juice

2 cloves garlic, peeled

1 tsp. salt

pepper to taste

½ tsp. ground cumin

3 tbsp. olive oil

2 tbsp. pine nuts

dash of paprika

2 tbsp. fresh parsley, chopped

raw vegetables (a selection of your choice)

pita bread

*You can use canned chickpeas in place of the dried ones. Two cups of canned chickpeas equals 1 cup of dried ones. If you use canned chickpeas, skip Steps 1–3.

1. Place dried chickpeas in a bowl, cover with cold water, and soak overnight.

2. Drain and rinse chickpeas. In a heavy pot, cover them with cold water. Bring to a boil, then simmer, partially covered, for about 1 hour. Add water as needed.

3. Drain chickpeas, reserving 1½ c. of liquid.

4. In a food processor, process the chickpeas with the tahini, lemon juice, garlic, salt, pepper, cumin, and ½ c. of the reserved cooking liquid. If hummus is too thick, add more liquid until it becomes pastelike.

5. Heat 1 tbsp. olive oil in a frying pan and brown pine nuts.

6. Serve the hummus on a large plate. Make a small dent in the center. Pour the remaining olive oil over the top and sprinkle with pine nuts, paprika, and parsley. Serve with raw vegetables and warm pita wedges.

Soaking time: overnight
Cooking time: 1 hour
Preparation time: 20 minutes
Makes about 4 cups

Lunch / Arukhat Tzohorayim

Although lunch can sometimes be a snack meal in the country, it is often quite a large meal—the main meal of the day—in cities and towns. Schoolchildren sometimes eat lunch as late as 2:45 P.M., when the school day ends, and some office and shop workers have a break of several hours during the day so that they can go home to eat. Dinner is often a light meal of salad and fish, usually eaten after 7:00 in the evening.

The aromatic sauce distinguishes this ground meat with sesame sauce entrée. (Recipe on page 47.)

Cheese Blintzes / Levavot Gvina

These pancakes are an Israeli version of a Russian dish. They are often served during Shavout (the Jewish Feast of Weeks), when dairy dishes are eaten, but they make a great vegetarian meal anytime.

Filling:

1 8-oz. package cream cheese, softened

1 c. (8 oz.) cottage cheese

1 egg

½ tsp. salt

½ c. raisins

Batter:

2 eggs

½ tsp. salt

1 c. water

1 c. all-purpose flour

6 tbsp. butter or margarine, for frying

sour cream, for topping

1. In a medium mixing bowl, make filling by combining cream cheese, cottage cheese, 1 egg, and salt. Beat until mixture is fairly smooth. Stir in raisins. Set aside.

2. In another bowl, beat 2 eggs well. Add salt and water and stir until blended.

3. Place flour in a large mixing bowl. Gradually add egg mixture from Step 2, beating well with a spoon to prevent lumps from forming.

4. In a frying pan or crepe pan, melt 1 tbsp. butter over medium-high heat. Stir melted butter into batter.

5. Pour ¼ c. batter into pan, quickly swirling pan so a thin, even layer covers the bottom. Cook on one side only, until batter is dry and surface begins to bubble.

6. Remove pancake from pan with a spatula and place on paper towels. Repeat with remaining batter, adding butter or margarine to lightly grease pan when necessary.

7. When all pancakes have been cooked, place 2 to 3 tbsp. filling on center of each. Roll up pancake and fold the open ends underneath.

8. Melt any remaining butter or margarine in the pan and quickly sauté pancakes over medium-high heat until brown and crispy. Serve immediately with sour cream.*

Preparation time: 20 minutes
Cooking time: 1¼ hours
Makes about 24 blintzes

*To reduce fat and calories in this recipe, use low-fat or nonfat cream cheese, cottage cheese, and sour cream, which are available at most supermarkets.

Melon Dessert / Liftan Melon

Israeli melons are small cantaloupe-style melons called Ogen melons. They are named for the kibbutz where they were first grown.

2 small cantaloupes

½ lb. green seedless grapes

½ lb. red seedless grapes

4 peaches

1 tsp. cinnamon

1 c. white grape juice

1. Cut melons in half. Scrape out and discard seeds. Cut out most of the melon flesh, being careful not to pierce the skin. Save the hollowed-out halves.

2. With a melon baller, scoop melon flesh into small balls, or cut it into small pieces with a sharp knife.

3. Wash grapes and remove from stems. Save 4 tiny clusters of red grapes for decoration.

4. Half fill a medium saucepan with water and bring to a boil over high heat. Carefully place peaches into boiling water and remove from heat. After 5 minutes, remove peaches with a slotted spoon. When peaches are cool enough to handle, peel and cut into small pieces.

5. In a large bowl, combine cinnamon, grape juice, melon, grapes, and peaches and stir. Spoon mixture back into melon shells. Top with reserved grape clusters. Refrigerate for at least 2 hours and serve cold.

Preparation time: 25 minutes
Chilling time: 2 hours
Serves 4

Bean Soup/Marak Shu'it

This simple soup is a wintertime favorite. Israelis use Egyptian field beans because they are the most easily available. The soup can be made with any kind of bean, however, such as navy or kidney beans.

1 tbsp. vegetable oil

1 onion, peeled and chopped

1 15-oz. can beans, undrained

1 6-oz. can tomato puree

2 10¾ -oz. cans (about 3 c.) beef broth*

3 cloves garlic, peeled and chopped

½ tsp. salt

¼ tsp. pepper

2 tbsp. chopped fresh parsley

3 c. water

pita bread

1. In a medium skillet, heat oil over medium-high heat. Add onion and sauté until transparent but not brown. Place onion in a large kettle.

2. Add beans, tomato puree, beef broth, garlic, salt, pepper, and parsley to kettle. Stir in 3 c. water.

3. Bring soup to a boil over high heat, stirring occasionally. Reduce heat, cover kettle, and simmer for 20 minutes.

4. Serve hot with pita bread.

Preparation time: 20 minutes
Cooking time: 30 minutes
Serves 4 to 6

To make this a vegetarian meal, substitute 2 cans of vegetable bouillon for the beef broth.

Ground Meat with Sesame Sauce/ *Siniyeh*

This dish, which is of Yemenite Jewish origin, is similar to the Greek dish called moussaka but uses tahini, instead of cheese, to make it kosher.

2 lb. ground lamb or beef

2 tbsp. chopped fresh parsley

2 onions, peeled and finely chopped

2 cloves garlic, peeled and crushed

½ tsp. cinnamon

½ tsp. salt

¼ tsp. pepper

2 tbsp. olive oil

2 tbsp. pine nuts

1 c. tahini, thinned according to directions on can

1. Preheat oven to 400°F.

2. In a large bowl, combine ground meat, parsley, onion, garlic, cinnamon, salt, and pepper. Knead to a paste with hands.

3. Brush a 9×9-inch baking dish with 1 tbsp. olive oil. Spread meat mixture evenly in dish.

4. In a small skillet, sauté pine nuts in 1 tbsp. olive oil over medium-high heat, stirring constantly, about 2 to 3 minutes, or until lightly browned. Remove skillet from heat as soon as nuts are cooked. Sprinkle nuts and cooking oil from skillet over mixture.

5. Bake meat for 30 minutes, or until brown on top.

6. Pour tahini evenly over meat and bake another 15 minutes, or until browned and bubbling. Serve with rice and salad.

Preparation time: 30 minutes
Baking time: 45 minutes
Serves 4 to 6

Baked Fish/Dag Bitanoor

Carp is a very popular fish in Israel. They are bred in carp ponds for European Jews, who like freshwater fish. (As a rule, Jews from other parts of the world do not like lake fish.) This recipe is also often used for cooking St. Peter's fish, which is found only in the Sea of Galilee (a freshwater lake). For this recipe, you can use flounder, sole, or haddock.

4 fish fillets, about 2 lb.

salt and pepper

1 medium onion, peeled and sliced

3 tbsp. butter or margarine

1 medium tomato, sliced

2 tbsp. fresh dill, chopped

2 tbsp. lemon juice

1. Preheat oven to 400°F.

2. Rinse fish under cold water. Pat dry with paper towels and lightly sprinkle with salt and pepper.

3. In a small frying pan, lightly brown onion in 1 tbsp. butter or margarine.

4. Spoon browned onion into casserole dish and spread evenly over bottom of dish.

5. Place the fish fillets on top of the onion slices. Then place the tomato slices on top of the fish.

6. Sprinkle the chopped dill over the tomatoes and dot with remaining butter or margarine.

7. Pour lemon juice over fish and bake for 15 minutes, or until fish flakes easily with a fork. Serve with salad and baked potatoes.

Preparation time: 15 minutes
Cooking time: 15 minutes
Serves 4

Poppy Seed Cake/Ugat Pereg

In Israel, one can always expect company, invited or not, after the Friday meal. This is a good cake to have on hand to serve visitors.

Batter:

½ c. milk

1 envelope active dry yeast*

1 tbsp. sugar

2 c. all-purpose flour, plus extra for rolling dough

½ c. butter or margarine, softened

1 12-oz. can poppy seed or prune filling

*If you use one of the quick-acting yeasts, follow package directions instead of the instructions given here.

1. In a small saucepan, scald milk over low heat and let cool slightly.

2. Warm a small cup by rinsing it in hot water and drying thoroughly. Combine yeast, 1 tsp. sugar, and 1 tbsp. flour in the cup. Add warm milk and stir until dissolved. Cover and set in a warm place for 20 minutes, or until mixture foams.

3. Beat together butter and remaining sugar until smooth. Gradually add remaining flour and yeast mixture.

4. Place dough on floured countertop. Knead for 15 minutes, adding enough flour to produce dough that is no longer sticky.

5. Place dough in greased bowl, cover bowl with plastic wrap, and set in a warm place to rise for 1 hour.

6. Sprinkle countertop with more flour. With a floured rolling pin, roll out dough into an 8×10-inch rectangle. Spread poppy seed filling over dough. Starting at one of the long sides, roll up dough, jelly-roll style.

7. Grease cookie sheet. Slide cake onto the cookie sheet so the seam is underneath. Cover cake with a damp towel and set in a warm place for 1 hour.

8. Preheat oven to 400°F.

9. Uncover cake, place it in the oven, and bake for 10 minutes. Reduce heat to 375°F and bake for 30 minutes, or until golden brown.

10. Remove cake from oven and let cool completely.

Frosting:

2 c. powdered sugar

1 egg white, lightly beaten

½ tsp. lemon juice

¼ to ½ c. water

1. To make frosting, sift powdered sugar into a mixing bowl. Make a well in center of sugar and pour egg white and lemon juice into it. Stir powdered sugar into liquid, adding water little by little until frosting is smooth.

2. Pour frosting over cake, letting it dribble down the sides.

Preparation time: 45 minutes
Rising time: 2 hours
Baking time: 40 minutes
1 cake makes about 30 slices

Holiday and Festival Food

For people of all ethnic groups, holidays are one of the most important occasions for families to gather together for the enjoyment of shared foods and traditions. Friends also visit each other during the holidays to share treats and good wishes.

Israelis come from all parts of the world, bringing with them a variety of savory recipes and interesting customs. The following recipes all have special connections to particular holidays or festivals, but many of them are also eaten year-round in Israel. Prepare these dishes for special occasions—or when you're just feeling festive. Then enjoy them amidst the warmth of family, friends, and good conversation.

Ginger gives teyglakh *its distinctive flavor. Top this holiday favorite with slivered almonds and glazed cherries. (Recipe on page 54.)*

Teyglakh

These honey treats are eaten on happy occasions, such as Rosh Hashanah, Sukkot, Simhat Torah, Hanukkah, and Purim.

Syrup:

1 lb. (1⅓ c.) honey

¾ c. water (plus more, if needed)

2 tbsp. lemon juice

2 c. sugar

Dough:

6 eggs

1 tbsp. ginger

½ tsp. salt

1 tsp. baking powder

3½ c. flour (plus ½ c. or more for rolling dough)

Garnish:

¾ c. slivered almonds

½ c. whole glazed cherries

1. Line 2 cookie sheets with aluminum foil and coat lightly with vegetable oil. Set aside.

2. In a large, heavy pot (at least 6-quart capacity), mix together the honey, water, lemon juice, and sugar. Heat to boiling.

3. While the honey syrup is heating, prepare the dough. Beat together the eggs, ginger, and salt until blended.

4. Sift together the baking powder and 3½ c. flour. Add to the egg mixture to form a sticky dough. Cut into 8 pieces. Dust each piece with flour and roll between your hands until it forms a roll about ¾-inch thick.

5. Slice each roll into 10 slices, ¾-inch thick. Add to the boiling syrup and simmer slowly for about 1 hour, stirring gently every 10 minutes. If the liquid seems close to evaporating, add more water, about ⅓ c. at a time.

6. Add the almonds and cherries during the last 10 minutes of cooking and stir frequently to make sure the syrup doesn't burn. The teyglakh will be a dark mahogany color.

7. When the cooking is complete, remove the pot from the heat. Immediately place the teyglakh, almonds, and cherries on the lightly oiled cookie sheets. Separate the teyglakh so they don't stick together. When cool, form the teyglakh into pyramids—one large or several small—and decorate with the cherries and slivered almonds.*

Preparation time: 40 minutes
Cooking time: 60 minutes
Makes about 80 individual pieces

*The teyglakh can also be rolled in chopped nuts or coconut
after they've cooled to make them less sticky. Teyglakh keep
well. To cover them for storage, use lightly oiled aluminum foil.

Sukkot Stew / Sukkot Tsimmes

A tsimmes is a fruit-and-vegetable stew eaten on the Sabbath and at Sukkot. This recipe combines many Eastern European traditions.

2 lb. chuck roast, cut into 1-inch pieces

1 tbsp. salt

2 tbsp. vegetable or olive oil

3 medium onions, peeled and sliced

2 large sweet potatoes, peeled and quartered

5 to 6 large carrots, peeled and thickly sliced

2 white potatoes, peeled and quartered

½ lb. prunes

½ lb. dried apricots

rind and juice of 1 orange

¼ c. brown sugar

dash of nutmeg

½ tsp. cinnamon

salt and pepper to taste

1. Sprinkle the meat with salt. Heat oil in a skillet over medium heat. Brown meat and onions.*

2. Add enough water to cover meat. Simmer, uncovered, for 1 hour.

3. Preheat oven to 350°F.

4. Place meat, onions, and cooking liquid in a 4-quart casserole. Add the sweet potatoes, carrots, white potatoes, prunes, dried apricots, orange juice and rind. Sprinkle with brown sugar, nutmeg, and cinnamon. Cover contents with water. Cover casserole dish and bake 1 hour.

5. Uncover, season with salt and pepper, and bake an additional 2 hours, or until the liquid disappears and the top turns crusty.

Preparation time: 40 minutes
Cooking time: 4 hours
Serves 6

*A nonstick vegetable spray may be used in place of oil for browning the meat and onions.

Potato Pancakes*/ *Potato Latkes*

The favorite at Hanukkah is probably latkes—potato pancakes fried in oil. The eight evenings of the holiday are traditionally a time to be with family and friends.

6 white potatoes

1 medium onion, peeled

3 eggs, beaten

¼ tsp. baking powder

½ c. matzo meal or flour

salt and pepper to taste

4 tbsp. olive or vegetable oil for frying

sour cream and/or applesauce, for topping

1. Peel the potatoes and grate. Drain any excess liquid. (This is important.)

2. Grate the onion and add to the grated potatoes. Add eggs, baking powder, and ½ c. matzo meal. Add more matzo meal if mixture is not thick. Season with salt and pepper to taste and blend well.

3. In a large, heavy frying pan, heat 4 tbsp. olive or vegetable oil until hot.

4. Using a large spoon or gravy ladle, spoon a portion of potato mixture into the pan and brown on both sides. Drain on paper towels. Repeat until mixture is gone, adding oil as needed. Serve hot with sour cream and/or applesauce.

Preparation time: 30 minutes
Cooking time: 40 minutes
Makes 18 large pancakes to serve 6 to 8

*For a healthier version of this recipe, use an egg substitute in place of the beaten eggs. Plain nonfat yogurt can be substituted for the sour cream, and you can use nonstick vegetable spray instead of oil to brown the latkes. For variety, you can also add grated zucchini, carrots, chopped parsley, or fresh dill to this recipe.

Haman's Ears or Haman's Pockets/Hamantashen

Dough:

⅔ c. butter

½ c. sugar

1 egg

½ tsp. vanilla extract

2½ to 3 c. sifted unbleached all-purpose flour

1 tsp. baking powder

dash of salt

Fruit Filling:

¾ c. pitted prunes

⅓ c. seedless raisins

¼ c. water

¼ c. shelled walnuts

¼ apple with peel

juice and rind of ¼ lemon*

2 tbsp. sugar

*Use a potato peeler or a zester to gently remove peel in small strips from the lemon. Try to avoid getting the white pith, which has a bitter taste. Chop or mince the peel with a knife for even smaller pieces.

1. Cream the butter and sugar. Add the egg and beat until smooth.

2. Add the vanilla. Stir in the sifted flour, baking powder, and salt until a ball of dough is formed.

3. Chill 2 to 3 hours or overnight.

4. For fruit filling, simmer prunes and raisins in water, covered, for 15 minutes, or until prunes soften slightly. Add nuts and apple. Grind or chop in a food processor. Add lemon juice and rind and sugar. Mix well. Refrigerate until ready to use.

5. Preheat oven to 375°F. Generously grease 2 cookie sheets.

6. Roll out ¼ of the dough on a lightly floured board until ⅛-inch thick. With a cookie cutter or empty can cut into 2-inch circles. Place 1 tsp. filling in the center of each circle.

7. Moisten the rim of the circles with water. Pull the edges of the dough up to form a triangle around the filling and pinch the three corners together.

8. Bake on a cookie sheet 10 to 15 minutes, until the tops are golden. Repeat with remaining dough.

Preparation time: 45 minutes
Chilling time: 2 to 3 hours
Baking time: 10 to 15 minutes
Makes about 36

Chicken Stuffed with Oranges/
Off Memooleh Betapoozim

This is an adaptation of a prize-winning recipe from a contest organized by the Israeli Touring Club in Jerusalem many years ago. It combines the most popular and economical ingredients in an Israeli meal: citrus fruit and chicken. The chicken can be served with matzo at Passover or with challah, a traditional bread, for a Sabbath meal.

1 2½- to 3-pound chicken

1 lemon

2 tsp. salt

1 tsp. garlic powder

2 tsp. paprika

1 tsp. chili powder

1 tsp. ground coriander

2 oranges

1 c. water

2 onions, peeled

*When checking chicken for doneness, it's a good idea to cut it open gently to make sure the meat is white (not pink) all the way through.

1. Preheat oven to 425°F.

2. Rinse chicken inside and out under cold running water. Pat dry.

3. Place chicken in a roasting pan. Cut lemon in half and rub one half over surface of chicken

4. In a small bowl, mix salt and spices together and sprinkle over chicken.

5. Squeeze juices from lemon half and from one of the oranges into roasting pan and add water. Place remaining orange, whole and unpeeled, in chicken cavity. Cut onions in half and add to the pan.

6. Cook chicken for 15 minutes, then baste with the pan juices and lower heat to 350°F. Cook for 1 hour, basting after 30 minutes.*

7. Remove orange from cavity of chicken. Cut orange and onions into wedges and serve with chicken.

Preparation time: 20 minutes
Baking time: 1¼ hours
Serves 4 to 6

Tu B'Shevat Salad

Salad:

1 endive

1 bunch watercress

½ head romaine lettuce

1 orange, peeled and cut into round slices

1 avocado, peeled and sliced

2 pitted dates, diced

¼ c. dried cranberries

1. Wash, separate, and shred greens. Combine into a salad bowl.

2. Add other ingredients.

3. Just before serving, pour dressing on salad and toss.

Salad Dressing:

¼ c. balsamic vinegar

1 clove garlic, peeled and crushed

dash of salt

1 tsp. honey

1 tsp. Dijon mustard

freshly ground pepper to taste

½ c. olive or vegetable oil

1. Combine all ingredients except oil.

2. Slowly whisk in oil and pour over salad.

Preparation time: 20 minutes
Serves 6 to 8

Noodle Pudding / Lokshen Kugel

It is traditional to eat dairy products at Shavout because historically it was the only time when grass was growing in the parched land, allowing chickens to lay more eggs and cows and goats to produce more milk.

½ lb. broad noodles

4 eggs

½ c. sugar

½ c. butter or margarine

8 oz. cottage cheese*

8 oz. sour cream*

1. Cook noodles according to directions on package. Drain.

2. Preheat oven to 350°F.

3. In large bowl, beat eggs, adding sugar a little at a time.

4. Melt butter in small saucepan over low to medium heat.

5. Add cottage cheese, sour cream, melted butter, and noodles to egg mixture and mix well.

6. Pour mixture into a greased 1-quart casserole dish and bake at 350°F for 45 minutes.

Preparation time: 25 minutes
Baking time: 45 minutes
Serves 4 to 6

*Low-fat or nonfat cottage cheese and sour cream, respectively, can be substituted.

Passover Popovers

These popovers make a festive holiday dessert when filled with preserves, stewed dried fruits, or sweetened whipped cream and nuts. They are also great for school lunches when filled with slices of meat, tuna, or cheese.

1 c. water

⅓ c. peanut oil

½ tsp. salt

1 c. matzo meal

4 eggs

1 jar fruit preserves, or 1 pint
    whipped cream, sweetened*

1. Preheat oven to 450°F.

2. In medium saucepan, bring water and peanut oil to a boil.

3. Add the salt and matzo meal and continue cooking and stirring until the dough no longer sticks to sides of pan.

4. Remove from heat and add unbeaten eggs one at a time, beating thoroughly after each addition.

5. Drop dough by the tablespoonful on lightly greased baking sheet and bake for 25 minutes.

6. Reduce heat to 325°F and bake 30 to 40 minutes or until browned.

7. When cool, carefully slit along one side and fill with fruit preserves or sweetened whipped cream.

*For a low-fat alternative to whipped cream, substitute a nondairy topping.

Preparation time: 20 minutes
Baking time: 1 hour
Makes about 12 popovers

Sabbath Stew / Dfina

Israel's many Jews eat slow-cooked stews on the Sabbath. Put in the oven on Friday before night-fall, the stew cooks overnight and is eaten for lunch the next day after the morning synagogue service. All of these stews contain meat and white beans of some type and are very nutritious. This version is characterized by the hard-cooked eggs, which will have delicious, creamy yolks from cooking so slowly.

1¼ c. (½ pound) chickpeas

1¼ c. (½ pound) navy beans

2 tbsp. vegetable oil or olive oil

2 large onions, peeled and finely chopped

8 small new potatoes, scrubbed or peeled

2 pounds beef (flank steak, short ribs, or brisket), rinsed under cool water and cut into 2-inch cubes

4 cloves garlic, peeled and finely chopped

1 tsp. ground coriander

1 tsp. ground cumin

1 tsp. allspice

8 uncooked eggs in their shells

1 tbsp. salt

½ tsp. pepper

1. Soak chickpeas and navy beans in separate bowls of water overnight.

2. Preheat oven to 375°F.

3. Heat oil over medium-high heat and sauté onions until golden brown.

4. Place onions, potatoes, and meat into a casserole with a tight-fitting lid. Add drained chickpeas and navy beans plus garlic, coriander, cumin, and allspice to the pot and mix.

5. Add the eggs in their shells and enough water to cover contents. If lid of pot does not fit tightly, put a layer of foil between pot and lid.

6. Bake stew for 1 hour. Stir in salt and pepper. Reduce heat to lowest setting and cook for 7 to 8 hours.

7. Remove eggs from shells and cut into quarters. Serve stew hot, garnished with egg.

Soaking time: overnight
Preparation time: 30 minutes
Cooking time: 8 to 9 hours
Serves 8

Index

About the Author

Josephine Bacon is an Israeli who lives in Anaheim, California. She has written about Israeli cooking for many publications, including the *Los Angeles Herald Examiner*. In addition to writing about food, Bacon is a professional Hebrew translator and courtroom interpreter and also teaches cooking at a community college in Southern California.

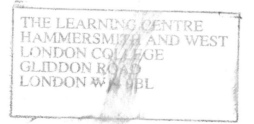
Photo Acknowledgments
The photographs in this book are reproduced courtesy of: © TRIP/S. Shapiro, pp. 2–3; © Walter and Louiseann Pietrowicz/September 8th Stock, pp. 4 (both), 5 (right), 6, 18, 39, 40, 45, 49, 52, 57, 58, 61, 62, 67; © Robert L. & Diane Wolfe, pp. 5 (left), 30, 34, 68; © Richard Nowitz/CORBIS, pp. 10, 15; © Hanan Isachar/CORBIS, p. 12; © TRIP/A. Tovy, p. 26.

Cover photos: © Robert L. & Diane Wolfe, front top; © Walter and Louiseann Pietrowicz/September 8th Stock, bottom left, spine; © Walter and Louiseann Pietrowicz/September 8th Stock, back.

The illustrations on pages 7, 8, 19, 27, 28, 31, 35, 38, 41, 43, 46, 50, 53, 55, 56, 59, 65, and 66, and the map on page 8 are by Tim Seeley.